WEATHER

IN FOCUS

CONTENTS

This edition published 1990 by
Franklin Watts
96 Leonard Street
London EC2A 4RH

ISBN 0 7496 0323 2

Original edition published 1988 by
Hobsons Publishing plc
Produced in conjunction with and sponsored by
The Meteorological Office

A CIP catalogue record for this book is
available from the British Library

Editor: Dr Kim Cross
Design: Ken Vail Studios
Designer: Pete Burclaff
Art Direction: Sally Moon
Graphics and illustrations by: Michael Badrocke, Paul
Cookson, Nick Hawken, Line and Line, Malcolm Ryan, Pete Burclaff

Acknowledgements
We are grateful to the following for supplying photographic
material:
p4/5   JFP Galvin; Crown Copyright reproduced with the
         permission of the controller of HMSO, Heather Angel
         Photo Library.
p6/7   JFP Galvin; Vaisala.
         Zefa photo library.
         K.E. Cross, Zefa photo library.

p8/9   University of Dundee.
p10/11   R Whyman, Kenneth Mylne, JFP Galvin, R.K. Pilsbury ERPS,
         Diana Wyllie.
p12/13   University of Dundee.
p14/15   Carol Unkenholtz, Tony Stone Picture Library.
p16/17   Science Museum Library, Tony Stone Picture Library,
         Crown Copyright reproduced with the permission of the
         controller of HMSO.
p18/19   Weathercall, The Meteorological Office, Crown Copyright
         reproduced with the permission of the controller of
         HMSO, Gabriella Jordon.
p20/21   Colorsport photo library.
p22/23   Wright-Rain, National Institute of Agricultural Botany,
         Womens Farming Union, Mary Evans Picture Library,
         Meteorological Office.
p24/25   John Laing PLC, Shell, Colorsport photo library,
         Meteorological Office, Crown Copyright reproduced with
         the permission of the controller of HMSO.
p26/27   Grampian Region Roads Department, Aspect Picture
         Library.
p28/29   BBC, Mary Evans Picture Library, The Meteorological
         Office, Crown Copyright reproduced with the permission
         of the controller of HMSO.
p30/31   CEGB.

We also acknowledge the following sources of information:

p5   Table after Shellard, H.C. in The Climate of the British
         Isles, ed. TJ Chandler & S Gregory Ch. 3 p. 71, Longman
         (1976).
p6   Illustration after Hardy, R; Wright, P; Gribbin, J; Kington, J
         in The Weather Book, p. 12, Mermaid Books (1985).
p7   Illustration after Perry, A H in The Climate of the British
         Isles, ed. TJ Chandler & S Gregory Ch 2 p. 9, Longman
         (1976).
p8   Illustration after Hardy, R; Wright, P; Gribbin, J; Kington, J
         in The Weather Book, p. 22, Mermaid Books (1985).
p10/11   Illustrations after Hardy, R; Wright, P; Gribbin, J; Kington, J
         in The Weather Book, p. 84, Mermaid Books (1985).

WEATHER

IN FOCUS

Dr Melanie Quin

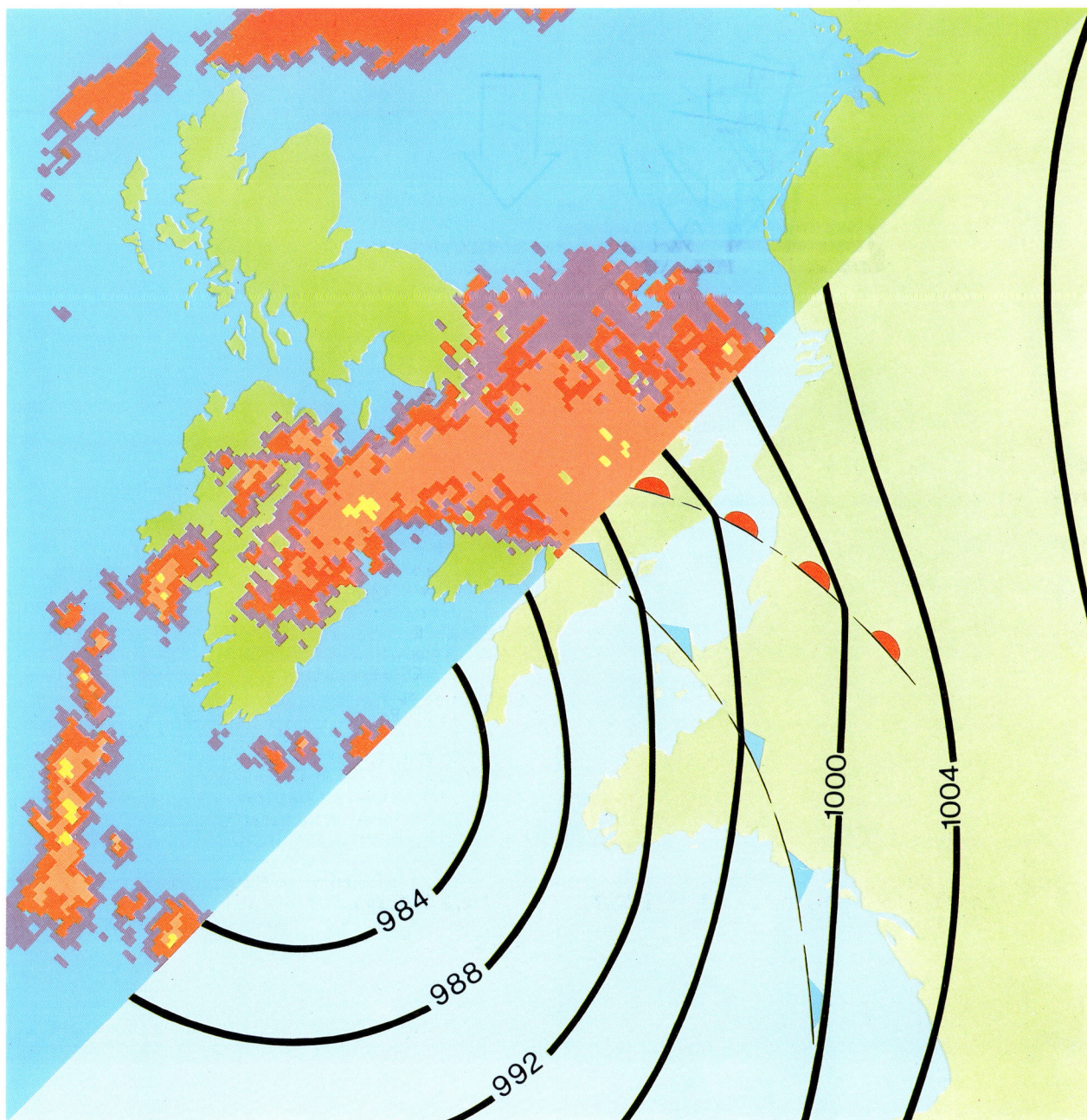

FRANKLIN WATTS

LONDON • NEW YORK • SYDNEY • TORONTO

MEASURING WEATHER

You can look at the sky, sniff the wind and listen to weather reports. But really to find out what's happening requires a weather station, equipped with the instruments to measure such meteorological variables as rainfall, temperature, air pressure, wind, humidity and sunshine.

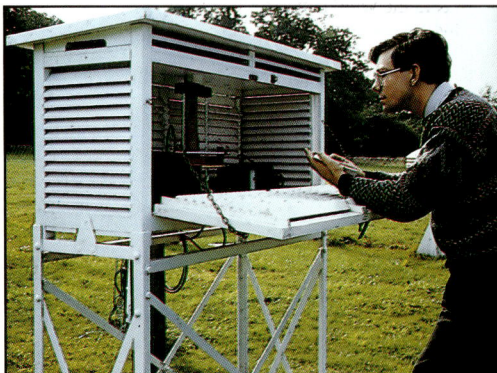

Thermometer screens

The weather is measured around the world, from London to Melbourne, and Tokyo to Mexico City. Accurate comparisons of data from different weather stations can be made if the measurements are taken at agreed times, using standard instruments and following standard procedures.

If you take a thermometer outside on a sunny day, the glass and metal parts will absorb the sun's radiation directly and be warmed to a temperature above that of the surrounding air. So standard **temperature** measurements are taken with thermometers housed in a **Thermometer Screen** – a louvred box that shades instruments from direct radiation but allows air to flow freely around them. (At home, without a **Thermometer Screen**, mount your thermometers on the north wall of the house.)

Maximum and minimum thermometers, checked and reset daily, record the maximum and minimum temperatures reached during a 24-hour period. A **thermograph** records temperature continually on chart paper wrapped round a rotating drum.

Air pressure changes with the weather. By monitoring pressure changes, and wind speed and direction, the coming weather can be anticipated. The **aneroid barometer** is a flexible metal box from which most of the air has been removed. As atmospheric pressure increases or decreases, the cylinder expands or contracts and a series of levers records the changes on a dial.

Since air pressure also depends on altitude, it is important to refer to a standard height.

Rainfall is collected in a **rain gauge** which measures the depth of rain water that would lie on the ground if none of it drained away or evaporated. Careful siting is important since the amount of water collected is affected by trees and buildings if they are too near.

The Campbell-Stokes recorder registers sunshine duration for one entire day. A glass sphere focuses the sun's rays and a scorch mark is burned on the recording chart whenever the sun is out. The length of the mark shows the duration of the sunshine.

Wind trace for 2.10–3.40am on 24 November 1978.

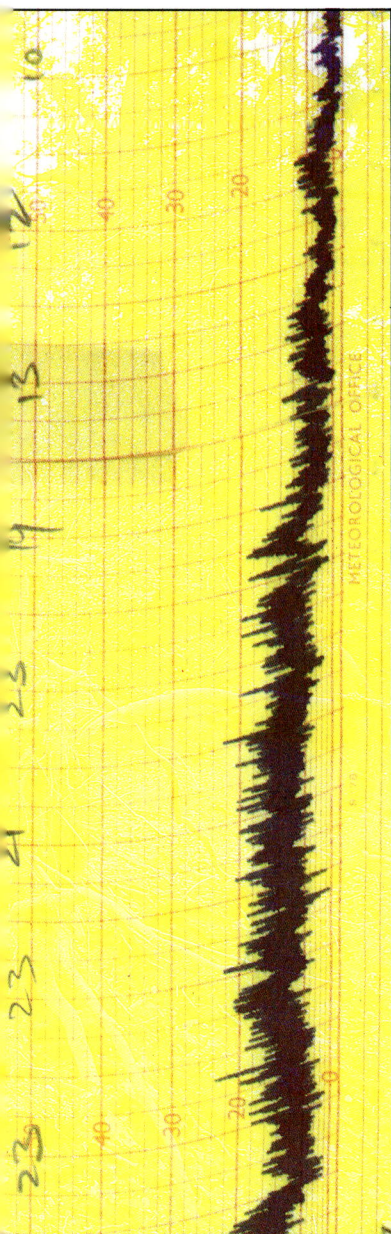

The anemometer (above right) measures wind speed. The Campbell-Stokes recorder (above) registers sunshine.

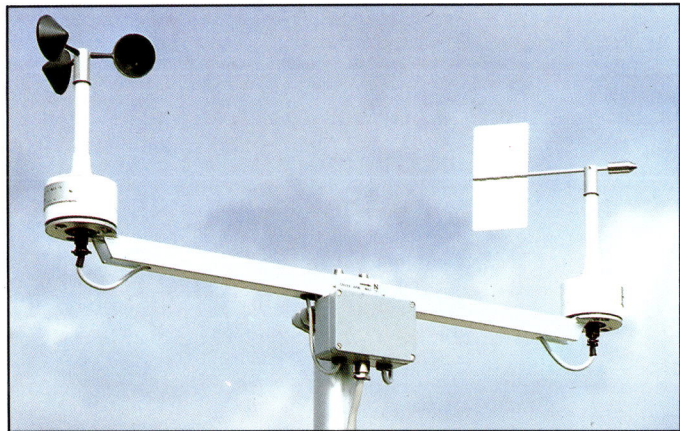

Humidity

Humidity is measured using two thermometers, one with its bulb dry, the other wet. As the water in the muslin evaporates, it draws heat energy from the wet thermometer and so the temperature reading falls. The moister the air, the less evaporation takes place and the smaller is the difference between wet- and dry-bulb temperatures. So a very humid day feels sticky, especially if it is hot as well.

The warmer the air, the more water vapour it can hold; when the atmosphere has absorbed as much as it can hold, it is **saturated**.

Relative humidity is the amount of water vapour actually in the air, expressed as a percentage of the amount of water vapour that could be held by the air at that temperature.

Wind velocity

Wind direction is measured with a **wind vane**.

Anemometers measure **wind speed**. The most common look like toy windmills. The three cups spin in the wind at a rate directly proportional to wind speed. This can be shown on a dial (like a car speedometer). Or it can be recorded continually, with the wind direction, on a chart to give a permanent record of the gusts and lulls that are caused by **eddies**. It is gusts that cause damage.

Variations through the day

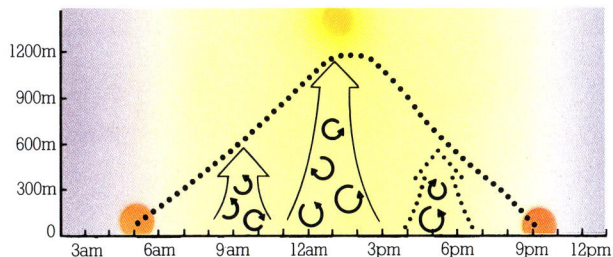

Sunshine is absorbed at the ground, which in turn heats the air immediately above it. Buoyant, heated air rises like smoke from a bonfire. Cool air sinks. One consequence of the heating of air by day and its cooling at night is a major variation in the wind between night and day.

It is often calm on a cool, clear morning – no wind blows.

As the temperature rises during the day, bubbles of warm air rise (known as thermals). They are replaced by air moving down from higher up. This subsiding air brings down stronger winds from aloft, in eddies. The wind measured near the ground is usually strongest in the afternoon. It dies down at sunset as the ground and the ground-level air cool and no more thermals are set up.

Wind speed changes with height from the ground. Above about 500m the wind flows freely. But the nearer you get to the ground, the slower the wind, because of frictional drag.

On cloudy days, variations through the day are far less marked, as the windspeed chart shows. Clouds block the sun's rays so thermals do not develop and mixing is due only to eddies caused by the roughness of hills and buildings.

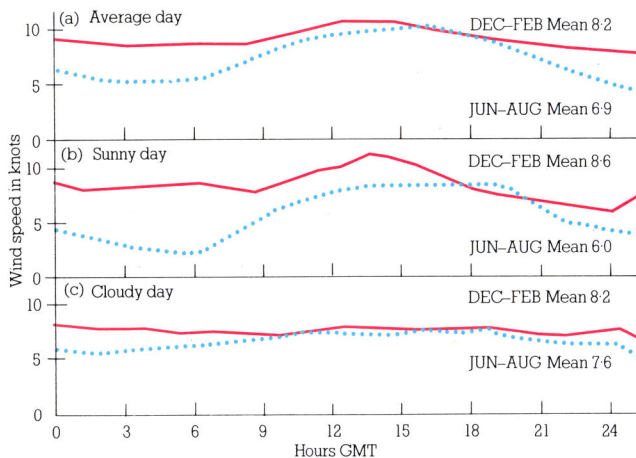

ACTIVITIES

► Visit a local garden centre or DIY store. What weather instruments are on sale for use in gardens? in greenhouses? indoors?
► How would you investigate the vertical variation of air temperature and wind speed in the first few metres above the ground? Why do you think temperature increases with height early on a clear, calm morning?

5

SUN, WIND AND WATER

The sun is the key to the world's weather since it is the source of all the energy in the atmosphere. It warms the earth's surface which, in turn, heats the air above. Heated air rises and colder air sinks to take its place. This simple flow takes place on all scales, from the global – air rises at the equator and subsides over the poles – to the local, as in land and sea breezes.

Seasonal changes occur as the earth moves through its yearly cycle. Variations in temperature set up horizontal pressure differences that make air move.

Water plays an important part in distributing the heat energy that drives the world's wind systems. Wherever water evaporates, over sea or wet land, heat energy is used. And the energy is later released through condensation, as in clouds and rain.

Sunshine and temperature

The proportion of the sun's radiation that is reflected back into space by the earth's surface – its **albedo** – greatly affects daytime temperatures. Fresh snow reflects 90% of sunlight, so very little heat is left to raise the temperature. In fact snow is melted more by the arrival of a warm air mass than by sunshine.

Sandy deserts have albedos of only 25%. There is little water to take heat for evaporation and little vegetation to use water and shade the ground. Hence the radiation is absorbed by the surface giving some of the highest temperatures found on earth.

Forests have an albedo of about 7% and use most of the incoming heat to evaporate water from leaves. When forest is cleared to leave bare soil, or to be replaced by pale-coloured crop land, the albedo is increased, less sunshine is absorbed and this change may raise temperatures, decrease rainfall and cause desertification.

Air masses

Large volumes of air moving round the world are often described as **air masses**. The characteristics of an air mass depend on where it has spent the last few days or weeks. If it has been over the equator it is warm; if over the poles – cold; over the sea – wet; over the land – often dry. The most interesting weather happens where air masses meet.

Polar continental air originating over Siberia is very cold and fairly dry. In winter it brings cold weather. More often our winter weather is brought by maritime air masses from the west – relatively cold (**polar maritime**) if from Greenland, relatively warm (**tropical maritime**) if from the Azores.

The earth traces an elliptical orbit round the sun.

Maritime air masses are also frequent (and relatively cool) in summer which is why we rarely have very high temperatures in western Europe. But occasionally **tropical continental** air does reach us, sometimes all the way from the Sahara. This brings gloriously hot, dry sunny weather – and newspaper headlines about heat waves – as during the summer of 1976.

The seasons

The intensity of the sun's radiation is constant through the year.

The seasons occur because the earth revolves about the sun with its axis tipped in relation to the plane of the orbit.

When the North Pole is tilted towards the sun, it is summer in the northern hemisphere and winter in the southern hemisphere. The opposite occurs six months later. The point where the midday sun is overhead varies between 23°27′N and 23°27′S – the tropics of Cancer and Capricorn.

Although summer is always warmer than winter, the particular weather of any season is modulated by the frequency of different types of **weather systems**.

Ocean currents

The winds drive the great ocean currents, but their direction also depends on the earth's rotation and the lie of the land. Huge masses of water are continually moving, sometimes warm (flowing to the poles), sometimes cold (flowing to the tropics). Warm and cold water heats or cools the air above it and so influences the climate. The UK is warmed by the **North Atlantic Drift** or 'Gulf Stream' (originating off Florida) and has a milder climate than Labrador, which is no further north but is cooled by a cold current from the Arctic ocean.

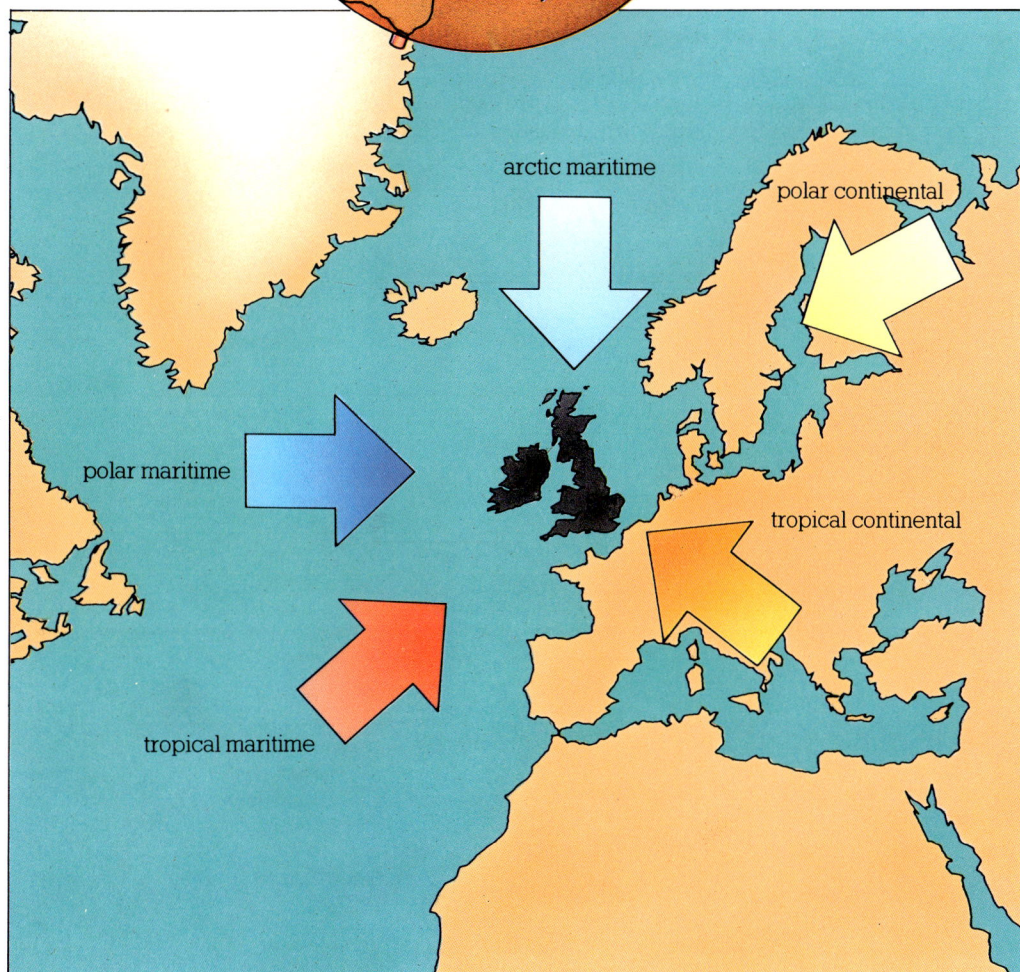

arctic maritime

polar continental

polar maritime

tropical continental

tropical maritime

ACTIVITIES

▶ **Imagine painting the Arctic black – what effect would it have on polar maritime air masses and world climate?**
▶ **Investigate albedo on a sunny day – open two umbrellas (one black and one light coloured) in the garden and place a maximum/minimum thermometer under each umbrella. You could try different-coloured umbrellas and make one wet, to investigate the effect of evaporation on temperature.**

Planetary-scale weather systems

Warm air rises, cold air sinks.

As hot, moist air rises at the equator, it flows polewards, cooling and losing water as rain as it goes.

Air, as wind, tries to flow directly from areas of high pressure towards areas of lower pressure. However the earth rotates beneath it and the **Coriolis effect** bends the winds to give the characteristic patterns shown in the picture.

At about latitudes 30° it begins to sink and flow back towards the equator. As it sinks it also warms, by compression (rather like a vigorously used bike pump). These areas of overturning air on either side of the equator are the **Hadley Cells**.

The tropical Hadley cell reaches much higher into the atmosphere than the polar cell.

In mid-latitudes, travelling **depressions** and **anticyclones** transfer heat. Warm air is pushed upwards and polewards ahead of a depression and cold polar air is dragged down to the tropics behind it. These swirling eddies of air are trapped between the warm air over the mid-Atlantic and cold air over the north Atlantic. They usually move towards western Europe.

High-level winds

Strong, high-level westerly winds or **jet streams** are often marked in satellite pictures by bands of high cloud circling the world. (Other clouds are seen to trace out the patterns of depressions.)

(1) Jet streams may circle the whole globe, with little north-to-south movement, giving changeable weather; (2) they may contribute to the development of fronts and depressions; or (3) disrupt into a stationary 'blocking' pattern that can produce either good or bad weather.

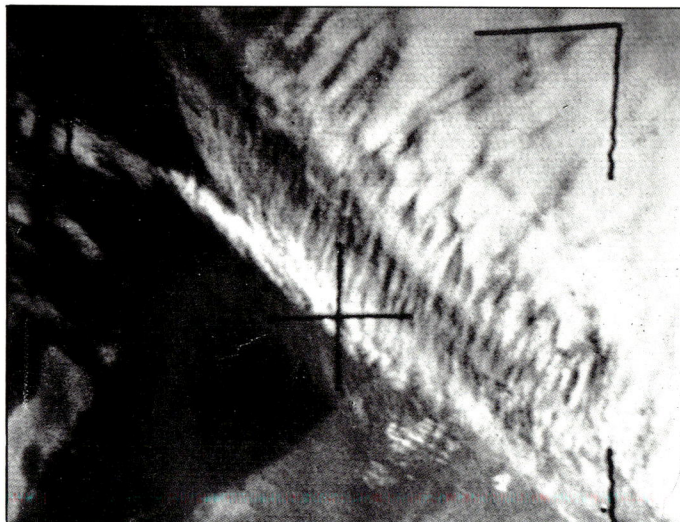

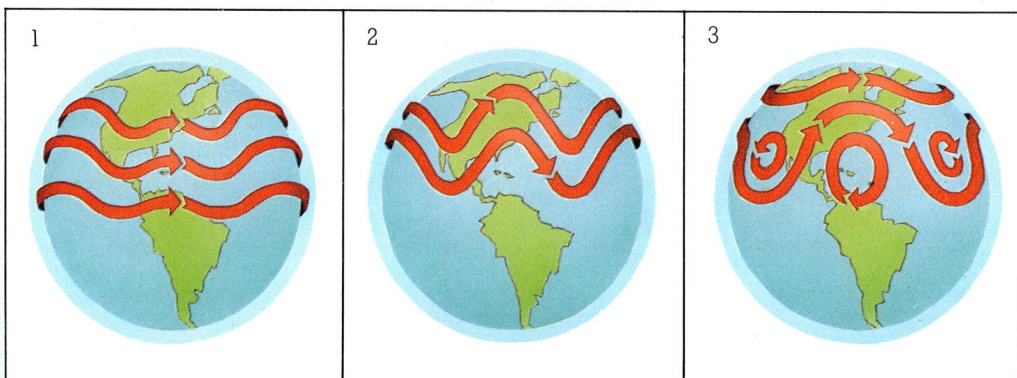

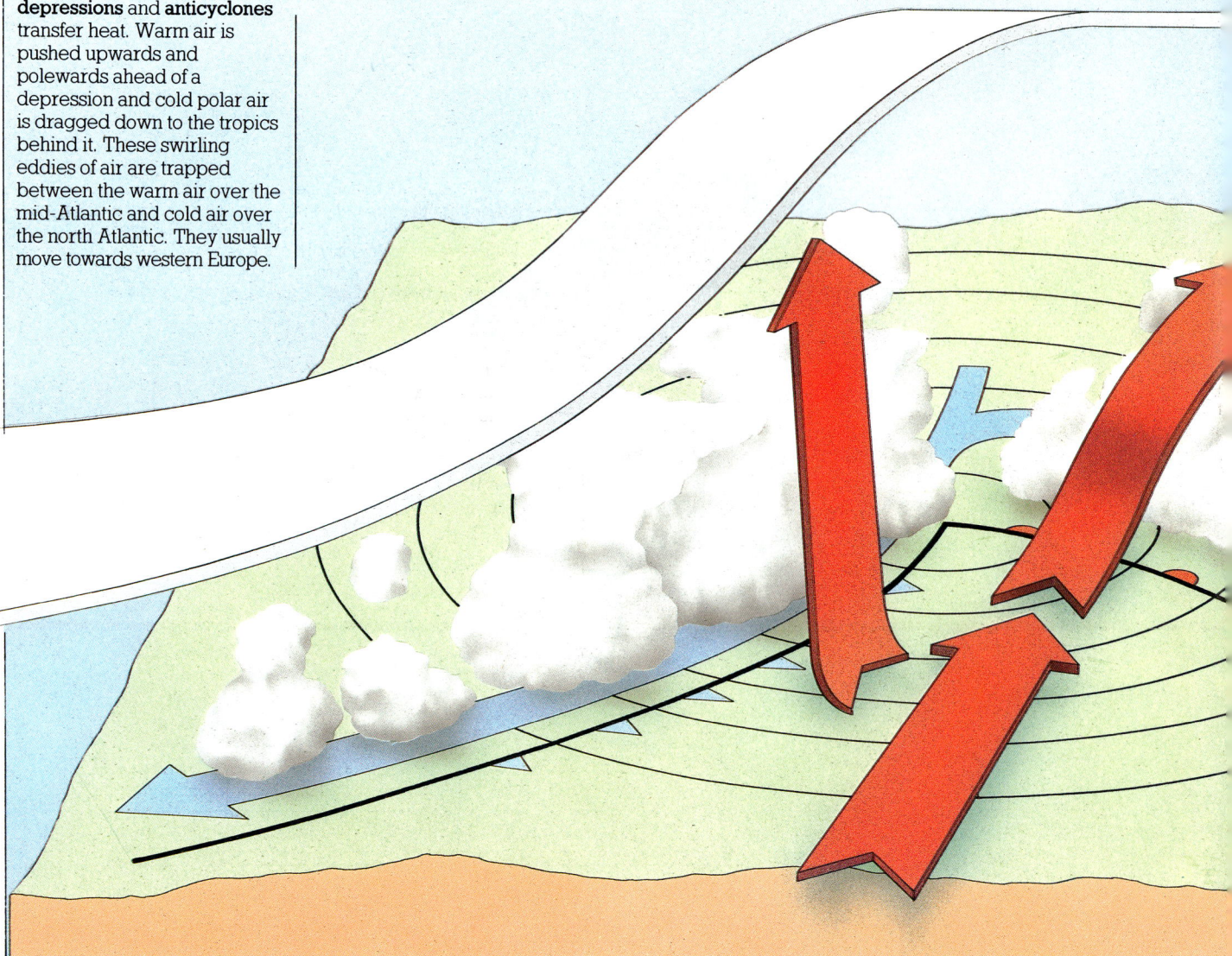

Jet streams are also very important in aircraft operations. Although they may be only 400km wide, they blow at up to 100ms^{-1} (220mph) and at about 10km above the Earth – at around standard cruising height. They were not discovered till World War II, when pilots of high flying aircraft found great differences between eastbound and westbound flight times.

The energy budget in the atmosphere

Over all latitudes between 40°N and 40°S, the earth's surface receives more solar radiation than it loses by direct radiation back to space. Because the earth is a sphere, air is warmed more at the equator than at the poles. If the heat stayed put, the tropics would get hotter and hotter, and the poles colder and colder.

Winds are the critical factor, taking hot air from the tropics and transporting it to the frozen polar regions.

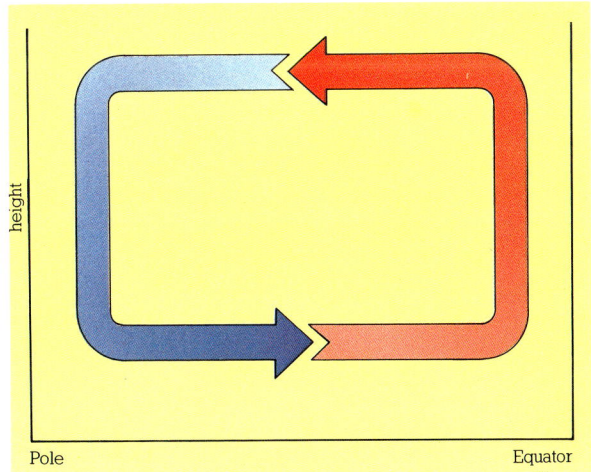

In the tropics, the trade winds dominate, blowing from the north-east in the northern hemisphere and from the south-east in the southern hemisphere.

The earth's energy budget

Only half the radiation coming in from the sun is absorbed at the earth's surface. 30% is reflected back (by clouds, by the earth's surface (albedo) or scattered back into space by air itself), and 20% is absorbed in the atmosphere.

The earth, being cooler than the sun, emits its energy in longer wavelengths (infra-red radiation) which bounce back and forth between the surface and atmosphere before being lost to space as long-wave radiation – only 6% of outgoing radiation escapes directly to space. The tendency of the atmosphere to prevent long-wave radiation escaping is called the **greenhouse effect**.

Warm 'tropical' air slithers gently up the warm front to middle levels; and rises up the cold front, in cumulonimbus, to join the fast-moving jet stream air. Cold air comes down behind the cold front.

ACTIVITY

▶ **If you took advantage of the jet stream on a flight from New York to London, how much quicker would your journey be than for an aircraft flying the Atlantic from east to west?**

What is a cloud?

A cloud forms when air has cooled enough for some of the water vapour it contains to condense out onto tiny particles of dust and salt in the air, and so to form water droplets or ice crystals.

In 1803, Luke Howard devised a scheme for classifying clouds into ten main types. Their Latin names combine the names of the three families of clouds (**cirrus** – curl of hair, **cumulus** – heap, **stratus** – layer) with information about their height above ground.

Cirrus clouds are wispy hair-like clouds often seen in the early morning.

Layer clouds (like the grey blanket of stratus cloud that often brings drizzle) are typical of hilly and maritime regions, and also a trough in a depression: they form when a large, spreading mass of warm air rises very slowly over a mass of colder air or over a mountain.

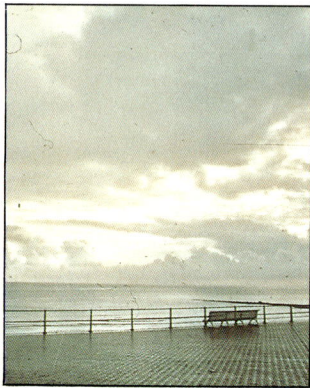

Heap clouds (like the cauliflower-topped cumulus clouds of sunny summer skies) form when bubbles of warm air rise quickly.

Cloud formation starts when a warm patch of ground heats the air immediately above it. This bubble of air is relatively warm and light, compared to the colder, denser air beside it, so it rises like a hot-air balloon. As it rises, it expands and cools.

When the air is relatively warm and moist and convection currents are strong, the bubble may rise faster and faster and the cloud may grow to a towering cumulonimbus. The drama of a thunderstorm – gusty winds, heavy rain, lightning and thunder – may last less than an hour, but produces the most spectacular weather.

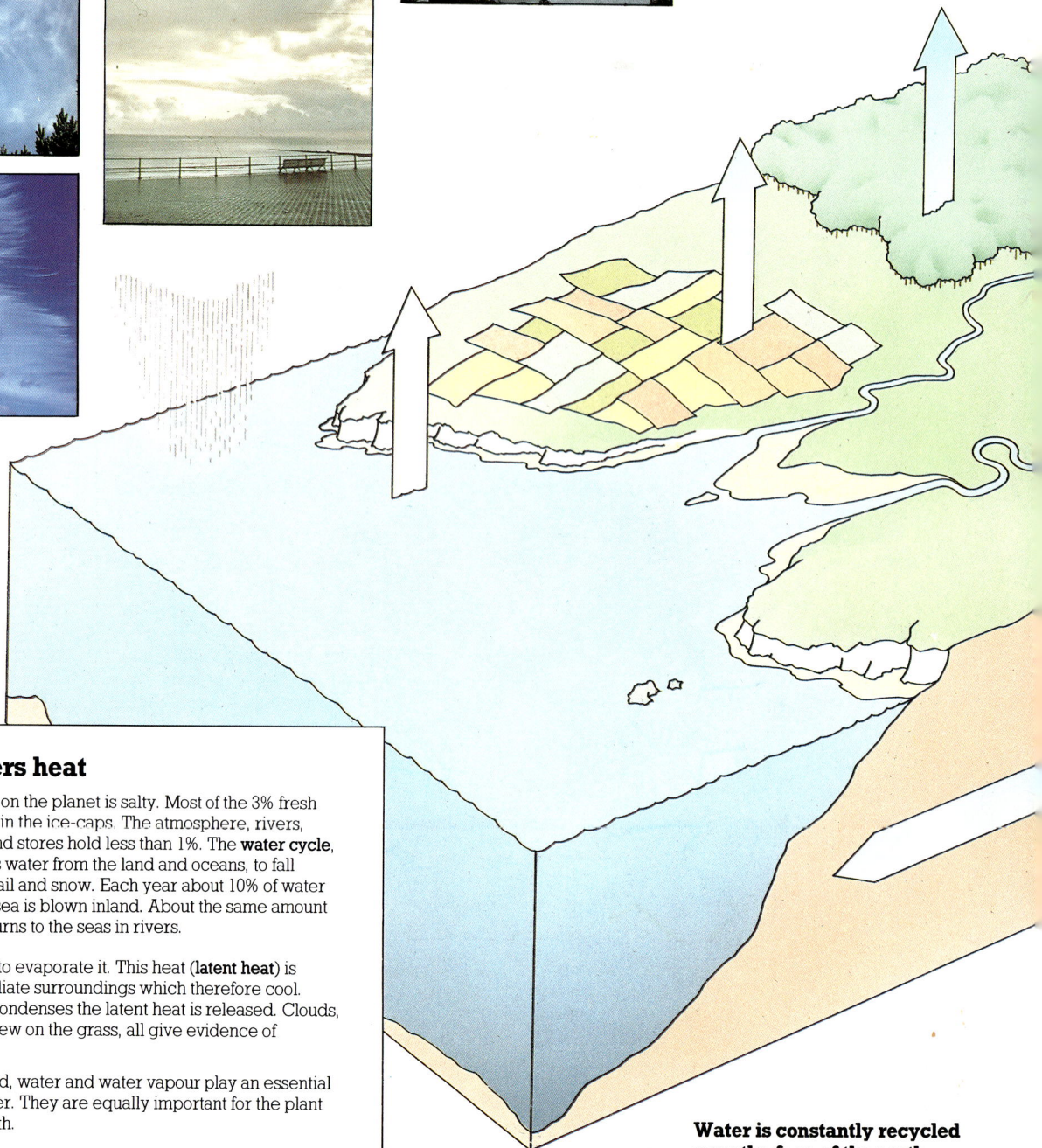

Water transfers heat

Over 97% of all water on the planet is salty. Most of the 3% fresh water is locked away in the ice-caps. The atmosphere, rivers, lakes and underground stores hold less than 1%. The **water cycle**, driven by the sun, lifts water from the land and oceans, to fall somewhere as rain, hail and snow. Each year about 10% of water evaporated from the sea is blown inland. About the same amount (some 40,000km^3) returns to the seas in rivers.

Water needs energy to evaporate it. This heat (**latent heat**) is taken from the immediate surroundings which therefore cool. When water vapour condenses the latent heat is released. Clouds, steam from a kettle, dew on the grass, all give evidence of condensation.

By moving heat around, water and water vapour play an essential part in making weather. They are equally important for the plant and animal life on earth.

Water is constantly recycled over the face of the earth.

Why does it rain?

Water droplets form whenever water vapour condenses. All clouds are formed of water droplets or large ice crystals that melt into drops as they are warmed. Each raindrop may contain about one million cloud droplets, to make it big enough and heavy enough to overcome the resistance of the air and to fall from the sky as rain.

But there is no rain without a cloud, and no cloud without rising air.

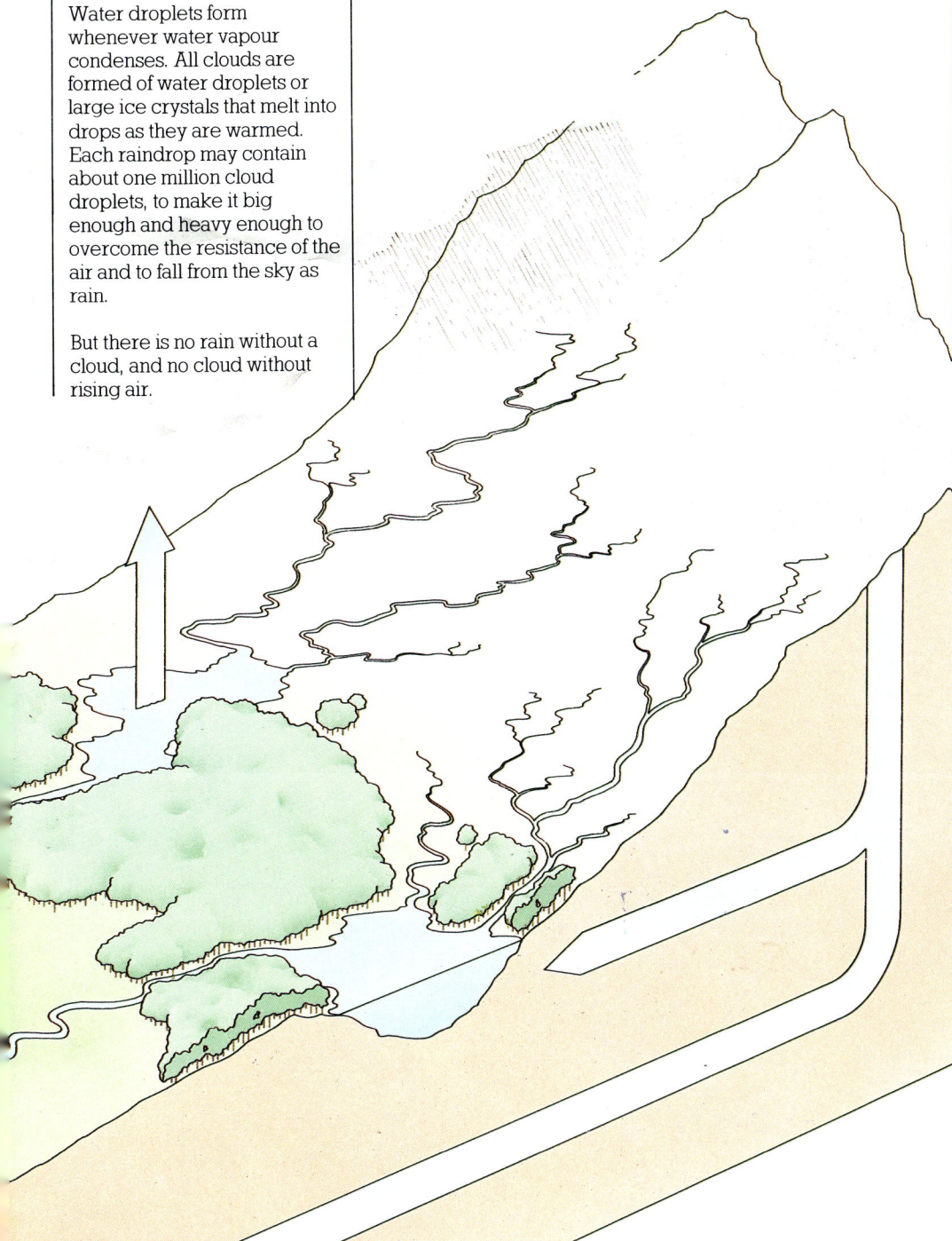

Rain shadow

The wetter areas of the country are associated with the direction of rain-bearing winds which rise over hills and mountains. So the wetter areas are in the west of the British Isles.

As moist air rises on the windward (western) side of hills, water vapour condenses and falls as rain or snow. As the air descends on the leeward side, it is compressed and warmed, and cloud evaporates and disperses leaving a dry **rain-shadow** area.

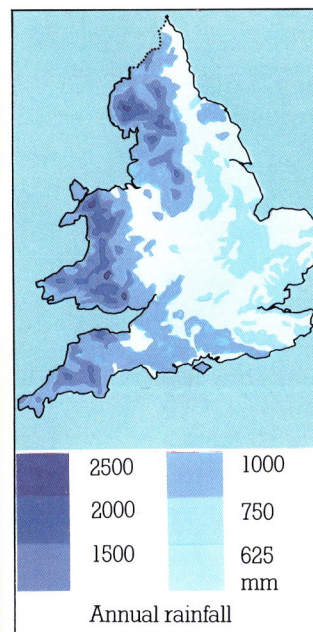

2500	1000
2000	750
1500	625 mm

Annual rainfall

ACTIVITIES

▶ If you hear a thunderclap ten seconds after you see a flash, how far away is the storm?
▶ Sometimes animals seem to sense thunder before you hear it – why should that be?

Thunder and lightning

Lightning occurs when a charge builds up in a thunder cloud. A leader stroke originates in the positive area and zigzags to the ground. It forms a path for the return stroke – a positive discharge from the ground to the cloud – which gives the flash of lightning.

The intense heating of the air makes it expand at great speed, producing the sonic bang we call **thunder**.

Lightning and thunder originate at exactly the same time, but light travels faster than sound.

The energy in a typical thunderstorm is enormous – equivalent to that released in a small atomic bomb.

Michael Faraday (1791–1867) discovered that electrostatic charges always collect on the outside of hollow containers. During thunderstorms, cars behave like **Faraday cages** – lightning travels over the surface of the vehicle and to earth – so people inside are quite safe.

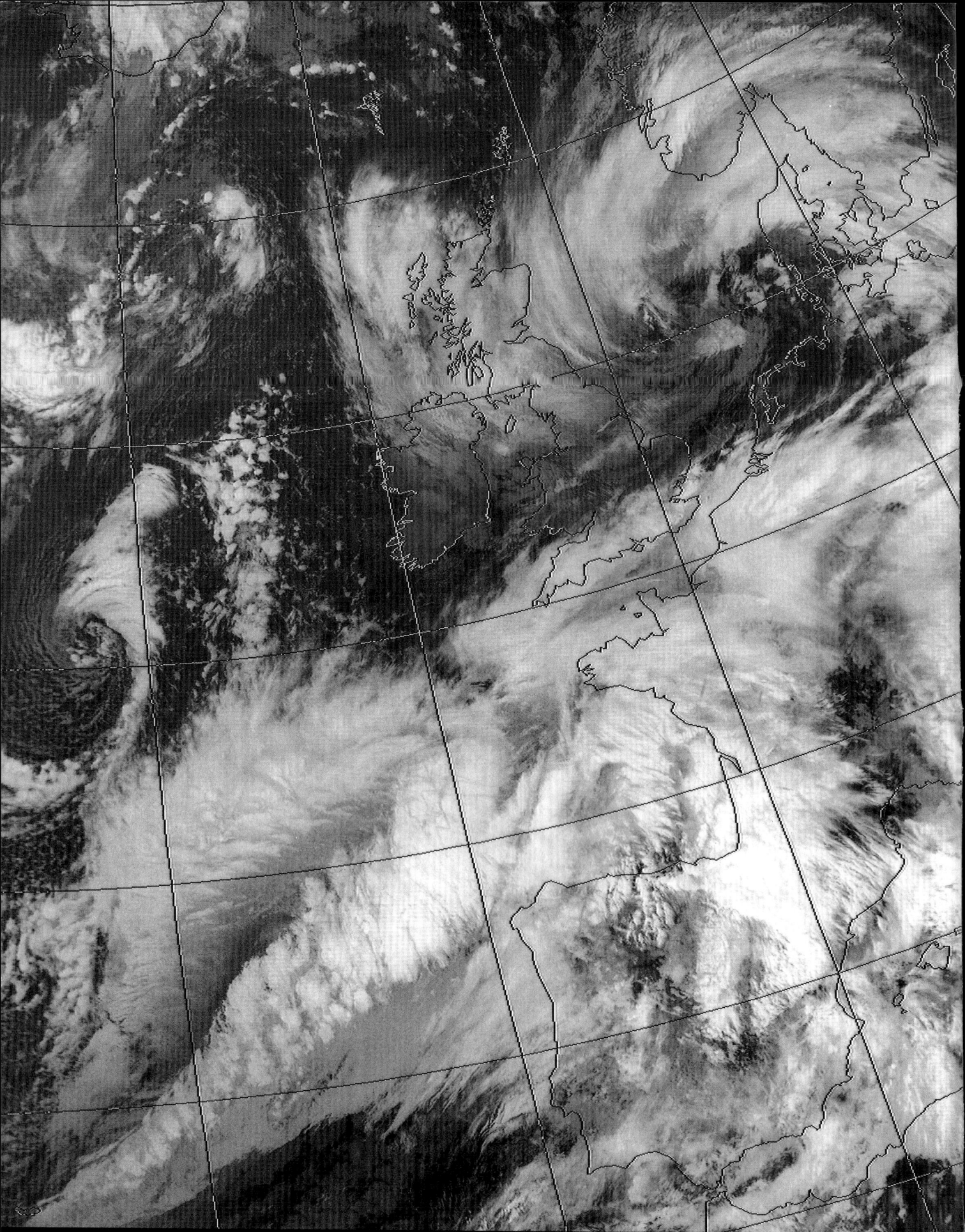

The storm of 15/16 October was a truly remarkable event. Although there have been many severe storms over the United Kingdom causing extensive damage, on this occasion the strength of the wind in the south-east of England, in October, made it an extremely rare event.

In these satellite pictures, high cloud, which is very cold, shows up as white areas while the dark areas indicate either warm sea or very low clouds.

15 October 1987 at 8.41am, the build up to the storm.

16 October 1987 at 2.36pm after the storm.

WATCHING WEATHER

There are about 7,000 weather stations around the world – in cities, at airports, at sea. Forecasters need information about the atmosphere all over the world, at surface level and upwards to at least 30,000–40,000 metres.

The weather knows no national boundaries and all countries co-operate in collecting and exchanging meteor-ological information. The World Meteor-ological Organisation (WMO) provides the international forum for agreeing standards, making practical arrangements and exchanging observations.

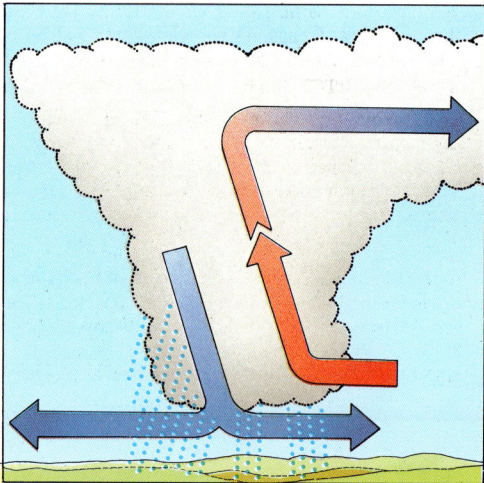

Aircraft data

Aircraft carry instruments that give wind velocity and temperature data along their flight paths. This is particularly valuable since airliners cruise at about the height of jet streams (10–13km).

The fully automated ASDAR (Aircraft to Satellite DAta Relay) system, installed on wide-bodied aircraft, provides measurements every 7.5 minutes. The data – wind speed and direction, air temperature, an index of turbulence, the aircraft's height and position – are extracted eight times an hour from the navigational system, and stored and transmitted every hour during level flight.

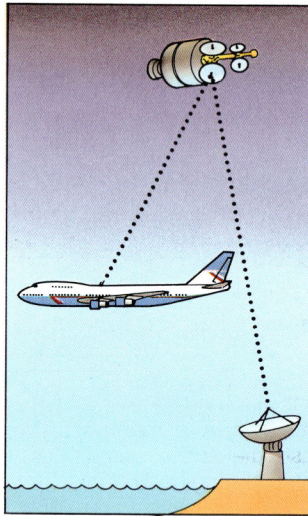

Growth of a Cumulonimbus cloud.

The cumulonimbus cloud is shaped like an anvil. Warm, moist air enters at the front, low levels, and rises towards the rear of the storm. Behind and under the updraught is the cool, dry downdraught. The cool air spreads out as it hits the ground: the forward-moving part helps to create new uplift at the storm's forward edge.

This type of radiosonde is expected to be introduced in early 1990.

Weather stations

Official observers in all countries record surface weather conditions at agreed times, using standard types of instruments located at approved sites.

On ice-caps, in deserts, dense forests and other sparsely populated places, automatic weather stations (AWS) have been set up. An AWS transmits information on pressure, temperature, wind and humidity. But instruments, unlike a human observer, cannot identify cloud types.

Time lapse photographs showing the life-cycle of a cumulonimbus cloud, photographed during the course of a summer after

Rainfall patterns

Because rainfall varies so much from place to place, especially near coasts and hills, rain gauges cannot give a full picture of what is happening. Weather radar provides the answer.

The rainfall radar beam scans horizontally. Any rain, snow or hail within about 150km reflects the signal, giving detailed information on the patterns of precipitation. Using rain gauges for calibration, the intensity of the radar echo can be related to the rate of rainfall at any place. Composite images from the network of weather radars can be used to monitor the advance of a band of showers or rainfall at a front.

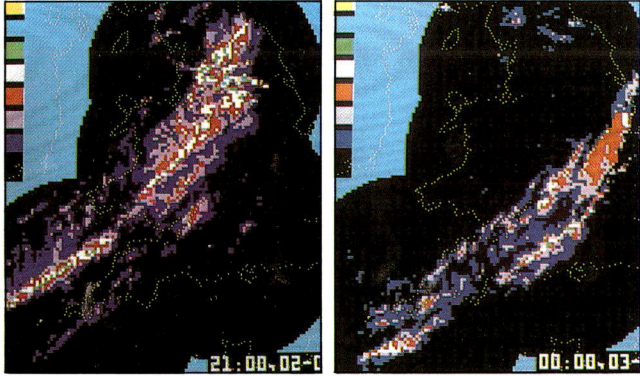

21.00,02-C   00.00,03-

Balloon soundings

The atmosphere is three-dimensional. What happens higher up affects the weather at the surface.

The best way to obtain measurements of temperature, pressure and humidity through the upper air is to release buoyant gas-filled balloons carrying recording instruments. The instruments take readings at frequent intervals and transmit the data to the ground.

The balloon also carries a reflective target for radar tracking. The radar signal bounces off this target, giving the height and position of the balloon throughout its ascent.

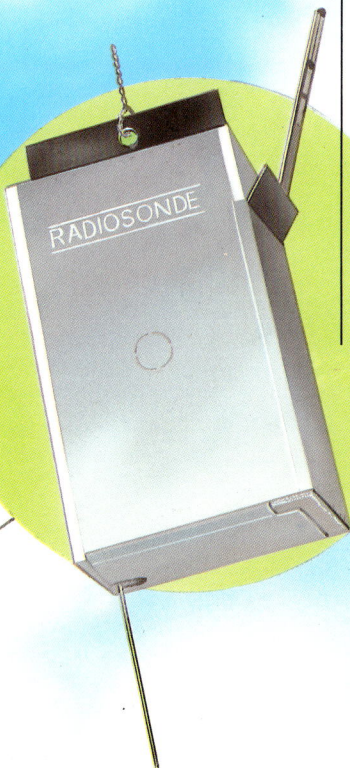

RADIOSONDE

ACTIVITIES

▶ **Many daily newspapers publish a weather chart reporting the positions of high- and low-pressure areas, and fronts. By collecting these over several days you will build up a 'time-lapse' impression of the movement of weather systems around the British Isles.**

▶ **How many do you need to make a weather flick-book?**

Meteorological satellites

Weather systems all have their own cloud patterns, and no two systems are ever identical. Satellite images reveal where – and what – cloud is present, giving detail that cannot be seen from the ground. They show forecasters what is going on, all over the world.
Satellites also locate, communicate with, and collect data from buoys, AWS, meteorological systems on ships, aircraft and balloons.

Geostationary satellites orbit at a height of 36,000km, above a particular point on the equator, where they have the same angular velocity as the earth. They monitor, continuously, a field of view that extends as far as the earth's curvature will allow – about 60° in each direction from their position above the equator. Their images are transmitted every half hour.

Polar-orbiting satellites circle at a height of 700–1,500km, and so provide more detailed global imagery. Typically, the satellite takes 100 minutes to orbit the earth (during which time the earth rotates through about 25°), and scans a succession of north-south bands.

Light- and heat-sensitive sensors emit simultaneous **visible and infra-red images** from meteorological satellites. In the visible, all areas of cloud, fog, sea, ice and snow show up because of their greater reflectivity. In the infra-red, the shades of grey from white to black represent different temperatures. High clouds are coldest and appear brightest, warm land appears black.

FORECASTING

A farmer on a hillside, within sight of the weather cock on the church steeple, may be able to predict the weather three or four hours ahead. Beyond that, to get it right 12 hours ahead, you have to look up to 3,000km away. To forecast a day ahead you need a hemispheric picture; to forecast three days ahead a global picture.

But this is not the whole story. Weather systems do not simply move. The atmosphere is interactive on a global scale and what happens in one area ultimately affects what happens everywhere else.

Information technology

Since Torricelli invented the barometer, meteorologists have been trying to explain weather conditions. And long before forecasts appeared on television, sailors and anyone whose work depended on the weather were making their own personal predictions based on experience and folklore.

In 1837, the electric telegraph was invented and it became possible to transmit information quickly from points around the country, to build up a picture of weather conditions further away, and so to make forecasts more than a few hours ahead.

Local newspapers carried brief weather reports from 1855, and by 1900 *The Times* was publishing regular weather maps.

Toricelli (below) and his barometer (right).

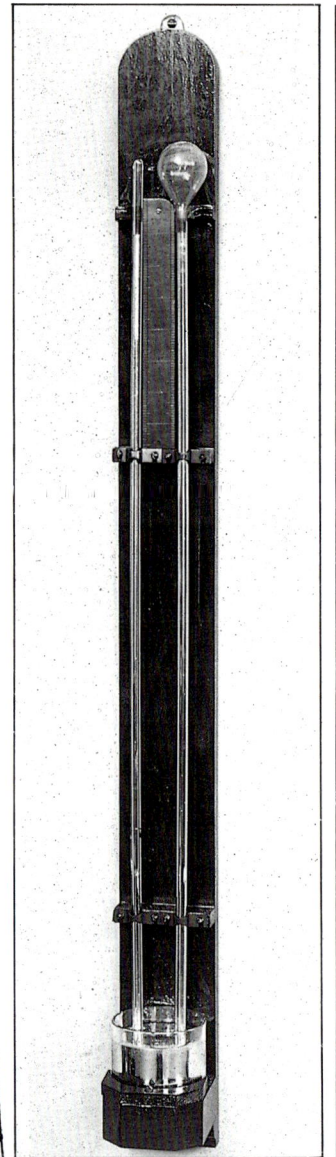

Correlation coefficient actual v forecast

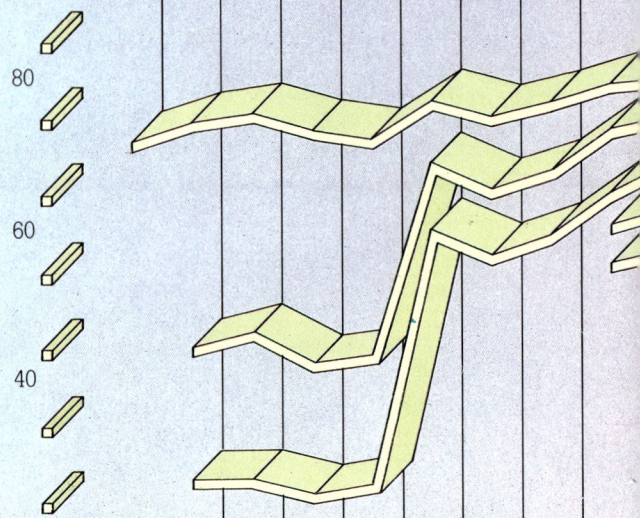

1968   70   72   74

80

60

40

How good are the forecasts?

'I got soaked – how can they say that it's an "isolated shower"? And they never predicted it would be so cold.

With all that computer equipment, you'd expect the Met. Office to get it right!'

The problem is that 'right' means different things to different people. Sailors and aviators, who are most interested in wind, find the 24-hour forecast to be right more than 85% of the time. A three-day forecast is rather less reliable, but still very useful for planning purposes: the success rate is about 80%.

For many people however, the most important element of the forecast is rainfall. In fact it is very difficult to predict the *amount* of rain. Also, whilst persistent drizzle might call off a day's sport, a single downpour giving the same amount would have little effect after dark.

A correct forecast of a showery day still doesn't mean that the forecaster can say exactly *who* will get a shower at *what* time. Accurate forecasting of individual showers is limited to only an hour or two ahead.

Numerical forecasting

Surface weather stations, ships, aircraft, satellites, radiosondes and radar all contribute to the global observing system that supplies the weather computers. Most measurements are **synoptic** (or 'seen together') and so observations from aircraft and satellites are adjusted to fit these standard times.

Computer forecasting programs start with all available data for wind, pressure, temperature and humidity, and convert them into values for regularly spaced **grid points**, at a fixed set of vertical **levels**. When the analysis is complete, the data are fed into a numerical model of the atmosphere.

The model is a system of mathematical equations representing all the important physical processes. It calculates the change that will occur at each grid point over successive intervals of about 15 minutes, through to eight days ahead. This computed forecast is evaluated and interpreted by an expert (human) forecaster.

Twice daily (based on the observations for 00.00 and 12.00 Greenwich Mean Time) numerical forecasts of the global weather are produced at the Meteorological Office, Bracknell.

Improvement in the accuracy of weather forecasts from 1968 to 1986.

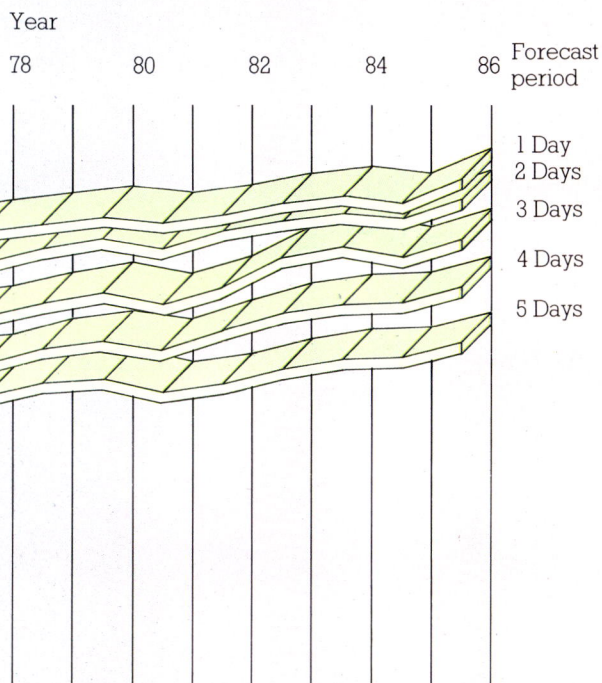

ACTIVITY

► Nowadays 'they' rarely get the forecast spectacularly wrong – but we certainly notice when they do. You can monitor the accuracy of Met. Office forecasts using instruments at your own simple weather station, and by cross-checking weather reports with the previous day's forecast.

FORECASTS FOR YOU

Weather forecasts are available in newspapers, on television, radio and by telephone. But they will be most helpful if you follow the weather through from day to day – by using the national and local forecasts and by making your own observations.

Here is the weather

Weather reports and forecasts are presented live on BBC **television** by the Met. Office weathermen, based at the London Weather Centre.

Live regional broadcasts – for three BBC regions and five ITV companies – are also made mostly by forecasters based in provincial Weather Centres. Other BBC regions and ITV companies receive Met. Office forecasts, either as scripts to be read by newsreaders or as personal briefings for the companies' own presenters.

There is a similar mix of live and scripted forecasts on national and local **radio** (both BBC and IBA), with regular national broadcasts direct from the London Weather Centre.

You will also find Met. Office 'pages' of up-to-date weather information on BBC's Ceefax and British Telecom's Prestel viewdata systems. Weather is one of the most popular services on viewdata and Prestel offers special 'pages' of information for farmers, pilots, sailors and holidaymakers.

The first television weather chart.

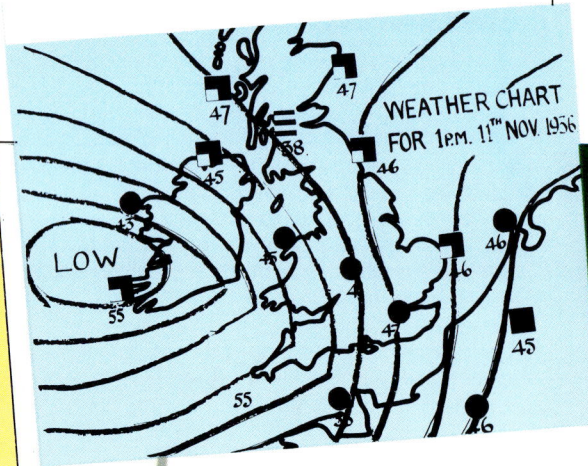

DETAILED WEATHER INFORMATION FOR EVERY REGION OF THE COUNTRY

Weathercall will provide you with the most accurate telephone weather forecasting service in Britain, available 24 hours a day, 7 days a week.
To get an individual local forecast for your region, dial 0898 500 followed by the 3 digit code indicated on the map. For a National 5 day forecast call 0898 500 430.
Each forecast is updated 3 or more times daily for up-to-the-minute accuracy. Information is supplied by The Met Office, the world leader in weather forecasting.

WEATHERCALL

The Weathercall service is charged at 38p per minute (peak and standard rate) 25p (evenings and weekends), including VAT

REMEMBER CALL
0898 500
FOLLOWED BY YOUR LOCAL NUMBER

All Weathercall information is provided exclusively by the Met. Office.

The Met. Office

WEATHER CHART FOR 1 P.M. 11ᵗʰ NOV. 1956

LOW

Weather charts

Isobars join points of equal pressure – the further apart they are, the lighter the wind – where they are close together the wind is strong.

The first **synoptic chart** was published by Elias Loomis, showing a storm which affected the eastern US in 1842.

The world's first television weather chart was broadcast by the BBC from Alexandra Palace, London, on 11 November 1936.

Today's coloured TV charts are familiar from breakfast TV through to the evening news programmes.

Bill Giles in action at BBC broadcasting house.

Science or confusion?

'*Cloud – 5/8 stratocumulus at 600m with 2/8 cirrus above*' makes no sense to the man in the street, but it's just what the pilot needs to know. The radio forecaster's job is to use simple language to give the impression this amount of cloud will make.

Equally, an exact measure of **visibility** is not likely to be useful unless it's very bad. But words like **clear** and **hazy** are helpful, and travellers, ramblers and hikers want to know when to expect mist or fog. Because the safety aspect is so critical, it is important to predict these conditions, and the popular definition of the words has become fairly well understood.

Planning the day

People use forecasts every day to decide what to wear, where to go, whether or not to take an umbrella. You might decide to have a picnic lunch, to cancel a barbecue, to spend the afternoon cycling or go to the cinema instead. Your knowledge and experience of the weather may help you work some local detail into the official forecasts. For example, cities create their own very special local climates. So if you live in a city, two factors to bear in mind are:

Gustiness – tall buildings and streets are far rougher, in terms of relief and contour, than most natural landscapes. This tends to channel winds and so increase their speed over very small distances. But over the whole town, average wind speed is lower than in the surrounding countryside because the buildings increase frictional drag.

Temperature – at night and in winter, urban areas act rather like storage heaters. This is the **heat-island effect**. The concrete, tarmac and brick of the city absorb heat during the day and release it slowly at night, quite apart from the heat generated by factories, offices and home central heating. Central London can be as much as 5°C warmer at night than surrounding countryside in Essex or Berkshire.

ACTIVITIES

► **National and local newspapers make use of the area forecasts and reports issued to the Press Association. New technology in newspaper printing now allows improved weather presentations. Which national papers are most informative? Which have the clearest graphics? Is your local paper taking advantage of the new technology?**

► **How many different symbols are used on the TV weather charts? Compare the presentation by national and regional television companies (if you get the chance, compare British TV weather charts with those on television in other countries) – what makes a 'good' chart and a 'good' weather presentation? What improvements would you make if offered the weatherman's job?**

Deluge at Wimbledon 1985.

FARMING TODAY

Farming is one of the most weather-sensitive occupations of all. Different crops are grown in different climatic regions around the world; and the yield of any one crop depends largely on the weather during its growing season.

European Community (EC) agricultural policies encourage farmers to minimise costs rather than maximise production. The role of the meteorologist is to help farmers work with the weather to produce a good harvest most cost-effectively.

Disease and pest warnings

Temperature, humidity and rainfall information are all used to prepare warnings of the animal and plant diseases and pests that multiply if conditions are favourable.

With meteorological advice, vets issue warnings of, for example, liver fluke and parasitic gastro-enteritis.

Warnings issued by plant pathologists and entomologists (who study plant diseases and insect pests) include potato blight, barley mildew, apple scab and pea moth. Acting on these warnings, farmers can apply pesticides to control disease outbreaks and save their crops.

An outbreak of disease can be more than a local problem: foot-and-mouth disease must be contained by quarantining cattle and disinfecting shoes and boots before leaving farm land. With airborne diseases, wind forecasts are important for predicting the likely spread. Low-level air trajectories ('flight paths') can be calculated from numerical forecast data and farmers alerted if their animals or crops are at risk.

The light aircraft that spray pesticides or fertiliser need local forecasts of cloud, visibility and wind to fly safely and operate effectively. If wind speed is not below a certain threshold, the spray will drift and may not reach the target crop. Different drop sizes can also be used,

Potato crop infested with potato blight.

depending on forecast wind speed and direction – large nozzles and low pressure on the liquid produces larger drops which fall faster and are less likely to drift.

'In the bleak midwinter . . .' the combination of strong winds, low temperatures and drifting snow can be fatal for exposed sheep. Weather warnings are often expressed in terms of **wind-chill** factors – for example, lamb wind-chill – determined through research on various species of livestock.

Changing the weather

Frost warnings are vital to many growers of fruit and vegetables. Frost damage to blossom in spring means a poor harvest of apples or plums in autumn. The forecast is therefore critical and precautions, though expensive, are worth taking.

If frost is forecast:

- windmills, or turbines, placed between trees can produce sufficient turbulence to bring down warmer air from above (remember, it is the ground that cools first)
- fires or oil burners, lighted in orchards, may be used to heat the air
- water sprays may be used on soft fruit – because water has a high **specific heat** it slows down the cooling and then, at freezing point, the released latent heat delays the frost even further.

Moisture in the soil

Irrigation is an expensive process, but well repaid in terms of crop yield (for example of potato and sugar beet). Meteorological advice on when to irrigate is based on weather forecasts for the next few days. Advice on how much water to use is based both on the amount of rain forecast, and on the soil moisture conditions – the result of accumulated effects of rain, sun and wind over many months.

In the longer term, strategic decisions about which crops to grow, which fields to plant them in, what irrigation equipment to buy and what size of water-reservoir to build, are also based on meteorological information:

- the expected rainfall for the region – including year-to-year variability
- the estimated growth prospects for the crop – comparing known climatic needs with observed, regional conditions.

Folklore or experience?

'Ice in November to bear a duck,
The rest of the Winter'll be slush and muck.'

'When Bredon Hill puts on his hat,
Ye men of the vale beware of that.'

Even today, when specialist forecasts have taken the place of folklore, experience of local conditions is invaluable.

In a hilly area, on clear nights, air may drain down slopes – cooling produces relatively denser, cold air that flows downhill and accumulates in valleys where it can result in frosts and fogs. Experienced farmers know the local frost hollows, and interpret weather forecasts accordingly.

Environments for farm animals

Meteorologists work closely with veterinarians to investigate weather-related agricultural and other problems.

Studies include monitoring the outdoor climate and indoor environments of naturally ventilated pig houses, chick-transporter lorries and cattle houses, leading to advice on, for example, the best site for a new cattle shed and on appropriate ventilation to keep the animals healthy.

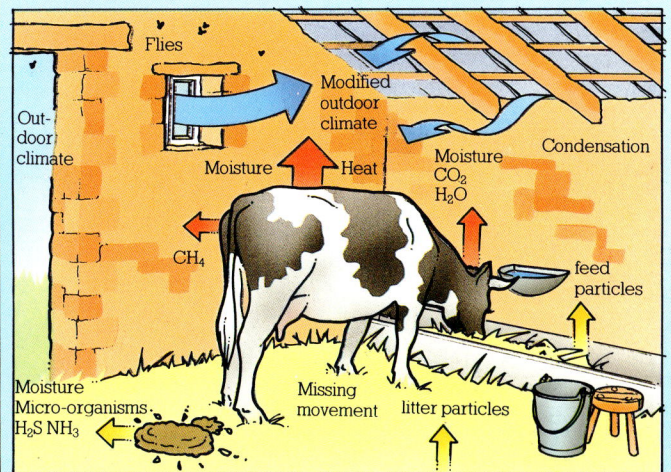

WORK AND PLAY

Weather forecasts are available through the media, or for the price of a telephone call. But the Met. Office also offers a range of consultancy services to paying customers who need detailed weather advice relevant to their specialist activities.

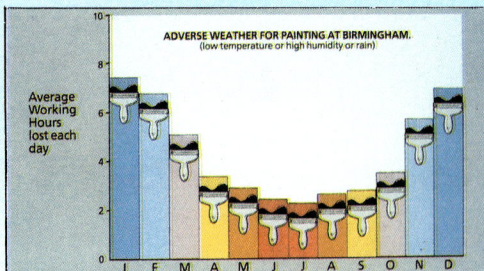

ADVERSE WEATHER FOR PAINTING AT BIRMINGHAM.
(low temperature or high humidity or rain)

Average Working Hours lost each day

J F M A M J J A S O N D

Construction-site operations

Whether the project is a high-rise office block, a new road or a shopping centre, weather is crucial before and during the construction period.

At the **design** stage, architects and surveyors make use of historical data to decide on site layout, building materials and the size of drainage and heating systems. Depending on the site's exposure to wind-driven rain, it may be worth building wind-breaks. The route of a new road may depend on the likelihood of fog in the areas of countryside it will pass through, avoiding a valley perhaps.

At the **planning** stage, and **on site**, contract and site managers base their decisions on specialist forecasts. Computer archives of past weather can be used to predict how much the weather is likely to interfere with outdoor work.

It is dangerous to operate tower cranes in high winds. Concreting is not possible during heavy frosts, and rain and snow can play havoc with project schedules. The Met. Office will supply site-specific advice 24 hours a day, for particular construction tasks, such as scaffolding, earth works and painting.

Offshore oil rigs

The very first surveys, the exploratory drillings, the towing out and erection of platforms and finally the full oil-production phase, are all extremely sensitive to weather and wave conditions.

One of the most serious hazards comes from long-wavelength (low-frequency) **swell waves**. These large waves are generated by storms thousands of kilometres away, and often arrive when the local winds are light.

Based on around 130 years of observations at sea – every detail extracted from ships' logbooks onto magnetic tape – the Met. Office can advise structural engineers on the likely extremes and will provide site-specific information, for daily operations. This includes:

- accurate daily forecasts of wind, waves and swell, with details on how local weather systems are likely to develop
- daily personal briefing by the local Met. Officer.

A particularly critical operation, such as towing out and mating the leg and hull sections of a platform, may require a **weather window** of calm conditions over several days. The latest weather advice is interpreted by a forecaster on the spot, working as part of the operations team and with a 24-hour hot-line to the offshore bench at the London Weather Centre.

Play abandoned

Detailed local forecasts can be important for people organising outdoor events such as fêtes, sports fixtures, pigeon racing and ballooning.

During the Wimbledon fortnight and the cricket season, rain is the critical weather element. If the grass is covered before rain falls, play can resume as soon as the rain stops (as long as the light is good enough). But wet or muddy ground needs time to dry.

The UK network of weather radars provides continuous surveillance. Composite images are used to monitor advancing shower clouds at frequent intervals – every 15 minutes is typical. By extrapolating the movement of a band of rainfall, a very short forecast is made, the covers put on in time, and disruption kept to the minimum.

The network of weather radars (pictured right) provides extremely detailed information.

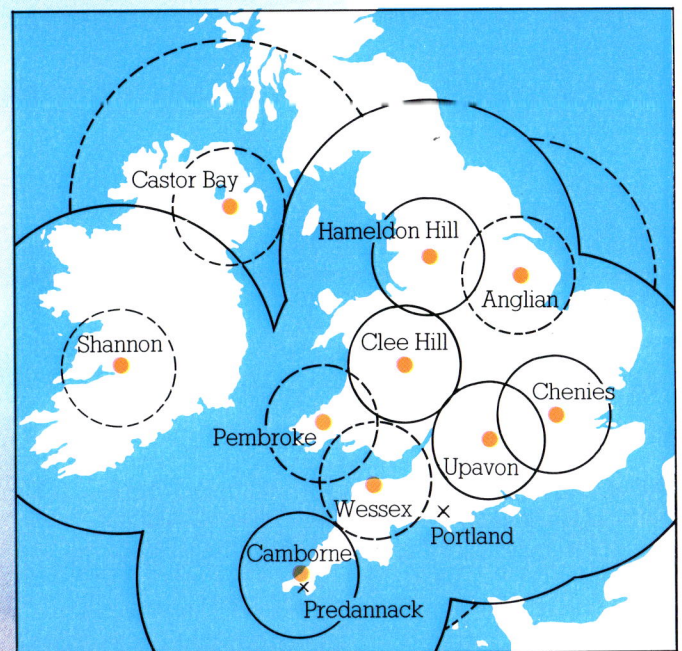

ACTIVITY

▶ How often during the football season does the pools panel sit to deal with Saturday's cancelled games? How much would it cost to insure against a cricket or golf match being called off? Or against a village fair being a complete washout?

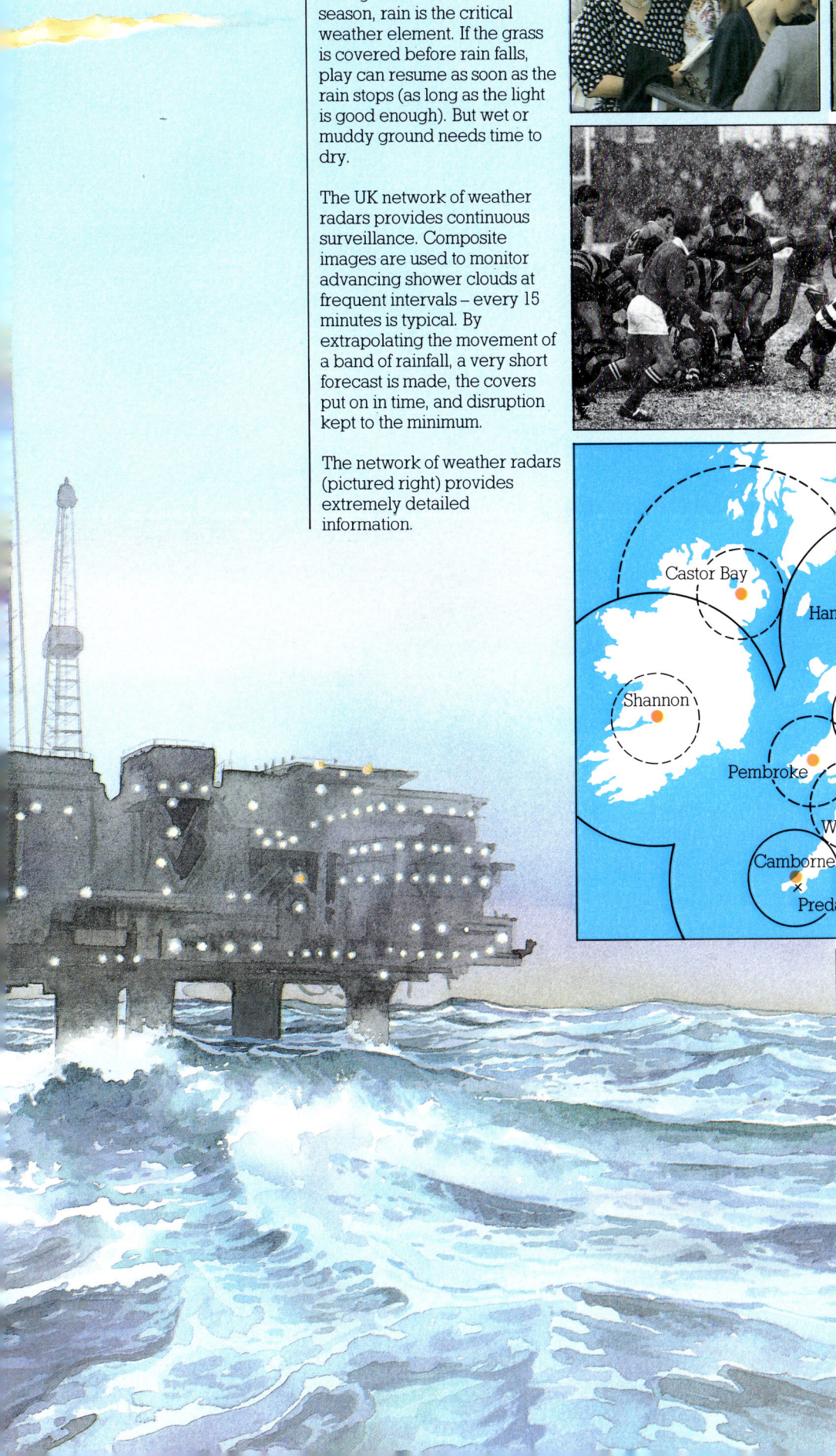

ROAD AND RAIL

On the road, heavy rain or fallen leaves may double or treble a car's stopping distance and upset handling. Iced-up points make chaos of commuter rail services. And snow upsets all communications, occasionally blocking roads and cutting off whole communities completely.

Road and rail transport are most vulnerable to winter weather conditions and there is no shortage of information and help for travellers.

Winter wisdom

One of the main problems of driving in falling snow is poor visibility. The other is the slippery road surface – cars tend to skid, but a bike in a skid can fall away under you. To stay in control, in snow as on ice, everything must be done in slow motion. The motoring organisations advise driving slowly in the highest gear possible, steering gently and avoiding harsh braking.

The winter sun is lower in the sky, and sun dazzle, especially off snow or ice, is an extra hazard.

Lighting-up times are given in the national papers. Extreme weather conditions, and details of road works and other transport problems are reported on local radio. Advice for drivers of juggernauts and small hatchbacks alike is: 'check the weather forecast before you go – if it's bad, ask yourself "Is this journey really necessary?"'

Keeping the roads open

The Department of Transport is responsible for the winter maintenance of motorways and trunk roads. They own a fleet of over 250 purpose-built snow-plough and spreader vehicles, and over 20 snow-blowers, operating from about 100 maintenance compounds on or near motorways.

Salt is used for de-icing almost the entire major-road network. The policy is to pre-salt roads when freezing weather or snow is forecast, to minimise the cost of snow clearing and reduce the risk of accidents. The decision to spread salt is taken by local authorities on the basis of the Met. Office **Open Road** specialist information service.

Many highway authorities have installed sensors in the road surface to supply data on temperature, wetness and salinity directly to local Weather Centres. Hour-by-hour forecasts of road conditions – in particular ice predictions – are made by computer, while radar images

provide up-to-the-minute information on the distribution of rain and snow.

Berkshire County Council used the Open Road service in 1986/87 and made 85 salting runs. Had the service not been available, they estimate an extra six runs, costing an extra £72,000 would have been made. Clearly an accurate forecast leads to savings in the winter maintenance budget.

Smog

Photochemical smog is caused by the action of strong sunlight on a mixture of nitrogen oxides and hydrocarbons emitted by industrial processes, from car exhausts and through combustion.

Smog is particularly bad in the Los Angeles Basin and Mexico City where local wind patterns and the surrounding mountains encourage the formation of **temperature inversions** – a layer of warm air overlies cooler air beneath and so traps pollution near ground level and prevents it from escaping. The smog is seen as a reddish haze during summer months.

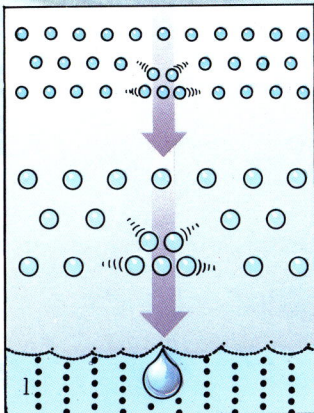

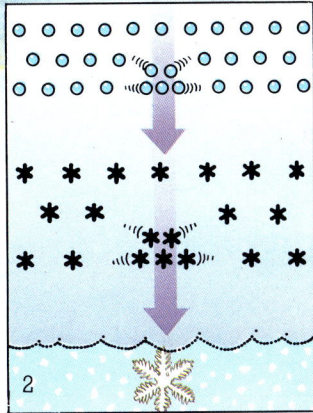

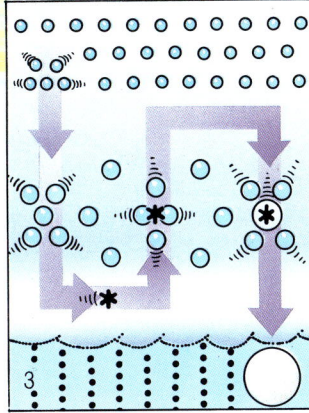

From droplet to potential hazard

Condensation occurs on cloud particles to form droplets, which merge to form larger **raindrops** (1).

In **snow** formation (2), microscopic ice crystals grow by condensation and cloud droplets settle and freeze onto them. The growing crystals form characteristic clusters which fall as snowflakes.

Hailstones (3) are made when raindrops in cumulonimbus clouds are carried up and down through layers of different water content. They collect fresh layers of clear or opaque ice until finally they fall out. (The strong up-currents can exceed 60 knots in a large cumulonimbus.)

Hail often occurs unexpectedly and can be almost blinding for drivers. But it doesn't usually last long, so motorists should slow down, turn on their lights and, if possible, pull off the road till the storm blows over.

Intercity and into town

In winter, the Met. Office gives British Rail warnings of ice and snow. These are particularly useful for Network South East, where ice on the conductor rail can cause severe difficulties and delay the heavy commuter traffic. Forecasts also allow snow-ploughs to be mobilised, and give advance notice of overtime work for maintenance crews.

In summer, forecasts of air temperature and cloud cover are made. Special patrols must be on the lookout for the buckling of continuously welded railway lines if high temperatures are expected.

The forecasts from computer models of the atmosphere are used directly in flight planning. They may also be used as input for further, specialist models – as when forecast surface winds are used to drive state-of-sea models.

Where you are interested in conditions on a small, local scale – as when hang gliding or wind surfing – you need the most detailed forecast available, and then need to interpret it for your area.

Land and sea breezes

This circulation between land and sea which reverses from day to night is of personal interest to those on holiday by the sea, whether boating, hang gliding or simply flying a kite.

Sea breezes occur by day when air is strongly heated over the land and rises, to be replaced by cooler, denser air flowing in off the sea. Sea breezes are strongest in the afternoon and may blow over 100km inland (though 20–30km is more typical in this country).

Land breezes occur at night when the land cools more rapidly than the sea. So air flows down the valleys and out to sea. The land breeze is usually less intense than the sea breeze.

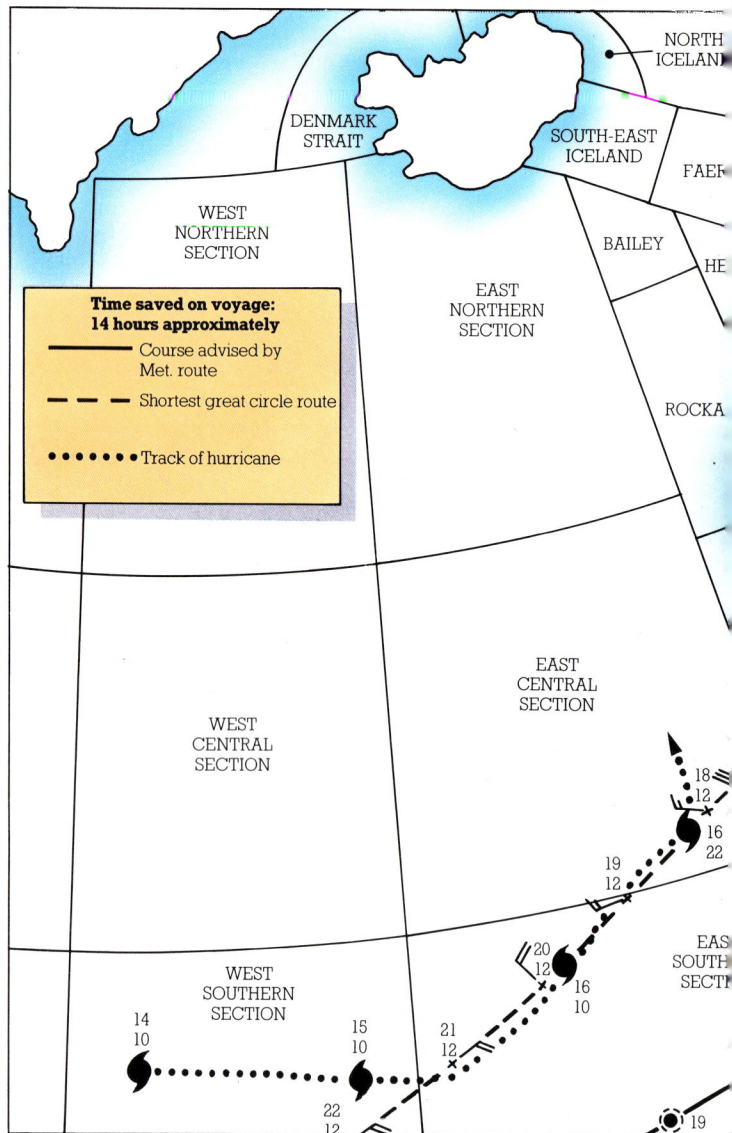

Forecasting for civil aviation

From take-off to landing, aircraft are subject to the weather and all its vagaries. Visibility, cloud height, turbulence and icing are all critical and conditions may be hazardous. Accurate meteorological information is clearly essential for safety.

The two World Area Forecast Centres (in Washington and Bracknell) compute global forecasts of winds, temperatures and other relevant information at all flight levels. These forecasts, usually up to 36 hours ahead, are distributed as a set of gridpoint values to Regional Area Forecast Centres (RAFCs) around the world, and direct to the airlines themselves.

The forecasts are also plotted on charts and provided as documentation to flight crews to advise them of the weather they will encounter *en route*.

Forecasters interpret the numerical forecasts and other information to produce **significant weather charts** showing, principally, jet streams and likely areas of turbulence and icing. The RAFC at Bracknell provides the significant weather charts for all flights westbound across the north Atlantic from airports in Europe.

Using weather forecasts improves safety records, and can help aircraft to make considerable savings in fuel by avoiding strong head winds and flying round instead of through storms, wherever possible. Savings to international civil aviation (through recent improvements in forecasts provided by Bracknell) amount to a staggering £56 million each year.

Time saved on voyage: 14 hours approximately

—————— Course advised by Met. route

– – – – – Shortest great circle route

• • • • • • Track of hurricane

NORTH ICELAND

DENMARK STRAIT

SOUTH-EAST ICELAND

FAER

WEST NORTHERN SECTION

EAST NORTHERN SECTION

BAILEY

HE

ROCKA

EAST CENTRAL SECTION

WEST CENTRAL SECTION

EAS SOUTH SECTI

WEST SOUTHERN SECTION

	0		2		4	
	Calm		Light breeze		Moderate breeze	
	Sea like a mirror		Small wavelets, still short but more pronounced. Crests have a glassy appearance and do not break		Small waves, becoming longer; fairly frequent white horses	
Equivalent speed at 10 m above ground in knots						
Mean	Limits		Mean	Limits	Mean	Limits
0	<1		5	4–6	13	11–16

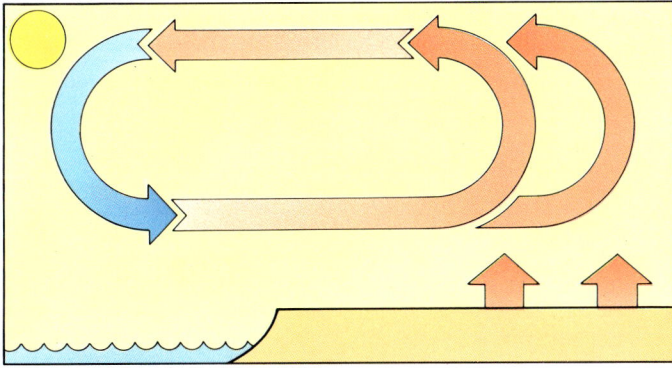

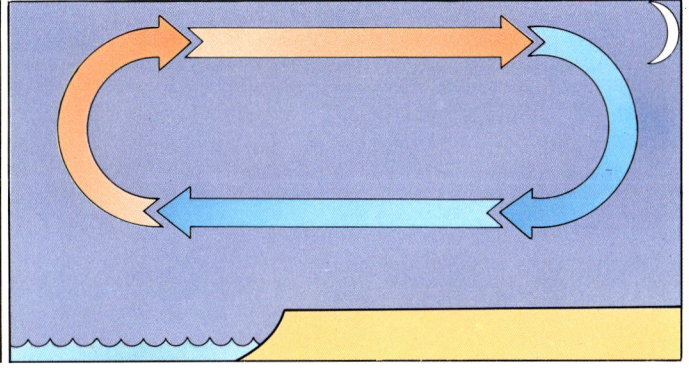

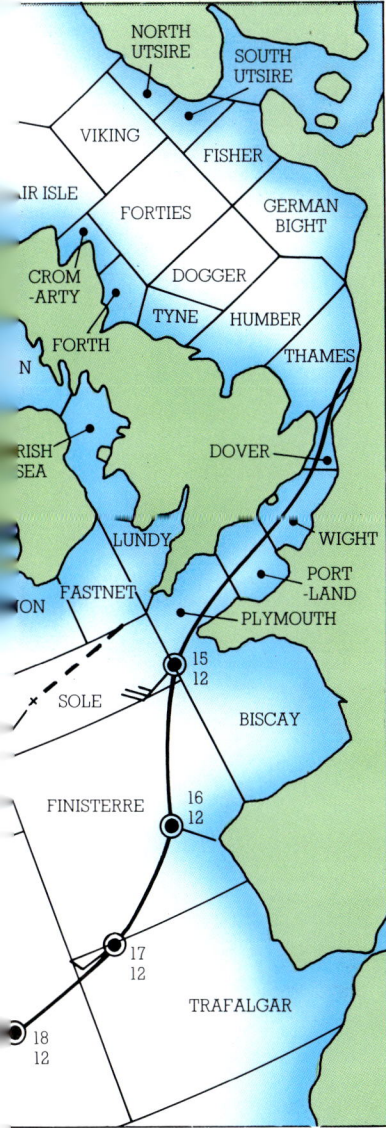

The Beaufort scale

It was the need to cut sailing times to the colonies and concern for the safety of ships that prompted the first meteorological services – giving warnings of storms at sea – around 1855. Today the global weather model is supported by a **global wave model**, **fine-mesh models** for accuracy on a smaller scale, and a team of experienced forecasters.

Forecasts of wind and waves expected over the major oceans are also used by the Met. Office to advise ships on the best route to take.

The weather analysis chart shows two comparative sea routes. It covers a voyage by a chemical tanker which left Rotterdam on 13 August 1986 bound for Trinidad. Following the recommended Met. route, the ship avoided the worst of the weather caused by remnants of hurricane *Claudette* and so saved about 14 hours. (Figures against charted positions show the date and hour of observations. The feathered lines indicate wind speed and direction to those points – a full stroke indicates ten knots, a half stroke five knots.)

The serious threat of tidal flooding in central London led to the building of the Thames Barrier at Woolwich. Forecasters use computer models of tidal flow to predict storm surges from forecast winds and pressures. The Storm Tide Warning Service provides extreme tide-level warnings to coastal Water Authorities; and to Thames Water for the operation of the Thames Barrier.

Dial before you sail and check the latest coastal weather conditions and high-water times anywhere off the UK. Marinecall forecasts are updated twice daily (three times in summer) and give information up to 20km off the coastline.

ACTIVITIES

▶ **What is your closest port or harbour? Find out which sea area forecast is relevant for the shipping offshore.**

▶ **If you were going wind surfing or boating, which Marinecall telephone number would you dial for your part of the coastline?**

6		8		10		12	
Strong breeze		Gale		Storm		Hurricane	
Large waves begin to form; the white foam crests are more extensive everywhere. Probably some spray		Moderately high waves of greater length; edges of crests begin to break into spindrift. The foam is blown in well-marked streaks along the direction of the wind		Very high waves with long overhanging crests. The foam, is blown in dense white streaks along the direction of the wind. The surface looks white. The 'tumbling' of the sea becomes heavy and shock-like. Visibility affected.		The air is filled with foam and spray. Sea completely white with driving spray; visibility very seriously affected	
Mean	Limits	Mean	Limits	Mean	Limits	Mean	Limits
24	22–27	37	34–40	52	48–55	–	>64

ENERGY MANAGEMENT

The gas and electricity industries have long made use of temperature forecasts to calculate energy demands over periods of a few days. More recently large stores and distribution industries have started using weather information to maintain stock levels, plan advertising and organise transport and distribution schedules according to the expected demand for, say, ice-cream.

The energy industry

Energy consumption – for lighting, heating, ventilation and cooking – is strongly affected by temperature, wind strength, sunshine and rainfall.

By acting on the Met. Office forecasts of these weather elements, the Central Electricity Generating Board (CEGB) and British Gas can anticipate the likely energy demand and make sure that it can be supplied efficiently. The forecasts give quantitative information at three- or four-hour intervals up to 36 hours ahead, with a further outlook.

Gushing gigawatts

It was 2.30am on 16 October 1987 when the hint of disaster first reached the 'quiet room' of the CEGB's National Control Centre in London. A 400-megawatt powerline between Southampton and Dungeness had tripped in high winds.

At 4am precisely, with hurricane-force winds battering the south-east, Britain's lifeline – the electricity power link with France – was lost. And so began the most critical six minutes in the history of 4800 miles of overhead lines and underground cables that make up our Super Grid.

The giant Dinorwig and Ffestiniog pumped-water storage power stations and the emergency gas-turbine stations were triggered into action. Only three circuits serving London were operational and one was 70%

overloaded. The voltage was reduced by 6% as one in ten homes in south-east England was cut off. Yet by 10am, power was again being bulk-supplied to every region in Britain.

Unlike gas, coal or oil, electricity cannot be stored in any quantity. By using weather forecasts electricity is generated most efficiently, leading to enormous (financial) savings. But the best weather forecast is not infallible. In times of crisis, only minute-to-minute balancing of supply and demand can maintain the national equilibrium.

The life of the British family is studied in detail by the CEGB. In winter, the minutes leading up to 5pm are critical – the time when industry and commerce are still working flat out and lights and heating are being turned on at home. The TV schedules also provide clues. The end of a popular programme or of the

They are made for a number of sites that are representatives of major urban areas.

Temperature and wind speed combine to give the wind-chill effect. This is probably the most accurate measure of how cold it actually feels. The Met. Office. supplies the Department of Health and Social Security with weekly data, to identify the periods of exceptionally severe weather when the elderly are given an extra fuel allowance.

Energy use varies with the weather. Gas, oil, solid fuel and electricity are all more in demand in the cold winter months.

Christmas Day power consumption for England & Wales (1,000,000,000 watts) (vertical scale)

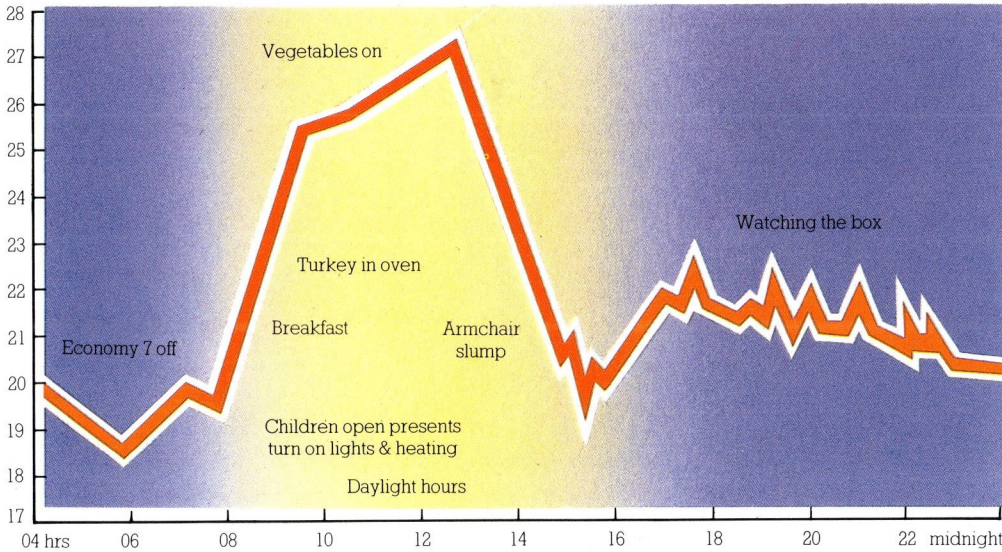

Vegetables on

Watching the box

Turkey in oven

Breakfast

Armchair
slump

Economy 7 off

Children open presents
turn on lights & heating

Daylight hours

04 hrs   06   08   10   12   14   16   18   20   22   midnight

feature film on Christmas afternoon produces a jump in demand – across the country loos are flushed causing water and sewerage pumps to switch on, and kettles are boiled.

This chart for Christmas day, 1987, shows that demand rose from the moment children began opening presents, through the time that turkeys were roasted and puddings steamed, till well-fed families went out for a walk or slumped in front of the TV. If it had been a white Christmas, demand would have been far greater.

ACTIVITIES

▶ The local council needs weather information all year round: rain and wind can make refuse tipping hazardous; in winter salt-spreading trucks (gritters) and snow-ploughs must be got ready.

Find out how often the council spread salt last year, and over the last ten years. What is the critical temperature? If you were in the planning department, how much salt would you order for next year? When would you stockpile, to be ready for winter conditions?

▶ If you do not plan ahead, the weather can upset heating and ventilation budgets.

Design an energy-efficient house for your part of the country. What fuel will you use for heating? Cooking? Other energy needs? Is your plan flexible enough to cope when a cold/hot/wet spell is forecast?

Glossary

Albedo:
The proportion of radiation from the sun that is reflected back by the earth's surface.

Air masses:
Used to describe the large volumes of air which move around the world. Air masses have different characteristics depending on where they have come from, eg., warm if they have been over the equator.

Anemometer:
An instrument that uses rotating cups, vanes and propellors to measure wind speed or force.

Anticyclone:
Area of high atmospheric pressure, usually accompanied by hot dry weather in summer and cold foggy weather in winter.

Barometer:
An instrument for measuring atmospheric pressure. It is used to forecast weather and to measure the height above sea-level. There are two basic types – mercury and aneroid.

Beaufort Scale:
Scale of numbers from 0 (calm) to 12 (hurricane) representing different wind speeds, together with a description of the corresponding land or sea effects.

Breeze:
A gentle wind of 4–31 mph, blowing from the sea by day, or from the land by night.

Campbell–Stokes recorder:
An instrument for measuring the amount of sunshine occurring in one day.

Cloud:
If air cools enough, some of the water vapour in the air will condense out as water droplets onto tiny particles of dust and salt present in the air. If it is cold enough, the water vapour condenses out as ice crystals.

Depression:
Area of low atmospheric pressure, with the lowest pressure at the centre, and usually accompanied by unsettled or stormy weather.

Eddy:
The name given to a small whirlpool, and used to describe a whirling movement of wind. Eddies are also found in fog or smoke.

Front:
The name given to the meeting point between two air masses at different temperatures or at different densities. At a cold front, cold denser air moves under warmer air, while at a warm front, warmer air pushes over and replaces colder air.

Greenhouse effect:
The atmosphere acts very much like a greenhouse trapping heat emitted by the earth.

Humidity:
The degree of moisture held as water vapour in the atmosphere. The atmosphere is saturated (100 per cent humidity) when it can absorb no more water.

Isobar:
A line joining points of equal barometric pressures.

Jet streams:
Strong, high-level, westerly winds, which blow at up to 100 ms-1 (220 mph) and at about 10 km above the earth. They are important for flying aircraft.

Radar:
Radar is short for RAdio Detection And Ranging. It gives the direction and distance of objects, by bouncing radio-waves off them and measuring the time it takes for the radio-waves to return.

Radiosonde:
A minature radio transmitter carried up in a balloon into the atmosphere, which broadcasts information about pressure and temperature etc back to a receiving station on earth.

Rain gauge:
An instrument for measuring the amount of rain that falls at a particular location. It measures the depth of rainwater that would lie on the ground if none of it evaporated or drained away.

Rain shadow:
An area that is shielded from rain by the local geography, such as mountains or hills.

Thermograph:
An instrument that records temperature continually on chart paper wrapped round a rotating drum.

Weather chart:
Diagram showing the state of the weather over a large area, such as the British Isles.

Index